AF131483

BOOK ANALYSIS

Written by Alice Cattley

Mansfield Park

BY JANE AUSTEN

Bright
≡Summaries.com

JANE AUSTEN

ENGLISH NOVELIST

- **Born in Steventon in 1775.**
- **Died in Winchester in 1817.**
- **Notable works:**
  - *Pride and Prejudice* (1813), novel
  - *Northanger Abbey* (1818), novel
  - *Persuasion* (1818), novel

Jane Austen was born in Hampshire in 1775, the daughter of an Anglican rector. Although the Austens had a modest income, Jane and her siblings were encouraged to read widely. She wrote her first spoof novella, *Love and Freindship* (1790) – misspelling deliberate – when she was just 14. Jane apparently read excerpts of the work aloud to her family, developing a writing style characterised by social observation and wit.

In 1801, Jane moved from Hampshire to Bath with her parents and sister Cassandra. Their life in the city was cut short, however, when her father died in 1805. Jane, her mother and Cassandra finally settled in the village of Chawton, where Jane wrote her most famous novels: *Sense and Sensibility* (1811), *Pride and Prejudice, Mansfield Park, Northanger Abbey* and *Persuasion.* In 1816, at the age of 41, she became ill and died the following year, possibly of Addison's disease. She continued to write until the very end and is buried in Winchester Cathedral.

MANSFIELD PARK

A STUDY OF FAMILIAL DUTY

- **Genre:** novel
- **Reference edition:** Austen, J. (2011) *Mansfield Park*. London: Penguin.
- **1st edition:** 1814
- **Themes:** class, family, marriage, propriety, slavery, acting, the home

Mansfield Park was written immediately after *Pride and Prejudice*. Considering the novels' proximity, readers may wonder at the difference between the two: while *Pride and Prejudice* is an homage to wit, *Mansfield Park* reveals the dark side of charisma, using Fanny Price as a foil to the glamorous Crawfords, whose clever conversation endangers those around them.

Of all Austen's novels, *Mansfield Park* arguably has the largest scope. The atmosphere of Mansfield Park itself – at once both stately and claustrophobic – is offset by the references to Antigua and the episode set in raucous

Portsmouth. The undertones of the slave trade add a political dimension that invites us to read the novel through a lens of power, control and freedom.

SUMMARY

FANNY ARRIVES AT MANSFIELD

The novel opens with the marriage of a young woman, Miss Maria Ward, to the wealthy Sir Thomas Bertram of Mansfield Park. The marriage is much discussed in the community, as Sir Bertram is socially superior to the Wards. Maria has two sisters, neither of whom make so advantageous a match: one marries a man named Reverend Norris, and the other, Frances, fares even worse – she marries a sailor, Mr Price, who is injured at sea and returns home a drunk. While Mr and Mrs Norris live near the Bertrams, the Prices are cast out as a familial embarrassment and live in Portsmouth. Mrs Price has no contact with her family for many years, until – pregnant with her ninth child – she writes a letter begging her wealthier sister for help.

Sir Thomas and Lady Bertram decide to send for the eldest Price daughter, nine-year-old Fanny, to live at Mansfield Park. The couple assumes Mrs Norris will be happy to have Fanny as a companion, but Mrs Norris – who is stingy and ungenerous

– insists the child will disturb her sick husband. When Fanny arrives, she is introduced to the four Bertram children: 17-year-old Tom, 16-year-old Edmund, 13-year-old Maria and 12-year-old Julia. She is scared of Sir Thomas and wary of her cousins, who largely disparage her for her lack of musical talent and inability to speak French.

Fanny does not adapt well to life at Mansfield. One day, Edmund discovers her in tears. He comforts her, bringing her paper so that she can write to her beloved older brother, William. From that moment, Edmund and Fanny become close friends. Although Maria and Julia are still dismissive, and Mrs Norris cruel, the rest of the family warms to Fanny. Sir Thomas decides to help William and helps him join the Navy. Five years later, Reverend Norris – who has long been ill – dies and his position as parish clergyman is handed down to Edmund. However, Edmund is not yet of age. Until he can take up the position, a man named Dr Grant and his wife move into the rectory. As Mrs Norris is now alone, the Bertrams again expect her to invite Fanny to live with her. To Fanny's relief, Mrs Norris insists that she is too poor and old to bring Fanny into society.

Another year passes, and Sir Thomas departs for Antigua in order to look after a plantation he holds on the island. He expects to be away some time. Though he regrets leaving his three youngest children, particularly his daughters, he takes Tom – who is in serious debt – with him in an attempt to straighten him out. Unbeknownst to Sir Thomas, his daughters are delighted that he is leaving; they believe his strict parenting gets in the way of their own pursuits. Fanny is not sorry to see him go either, but her sense of gratitude causes her pain and she "grieve[s] because she [cannot] grieve" for his absence (p. 31).

SIR THOMAS'S ABSENCE

With his father and older brother gone, Edmund takes over as head of the family. He notices that Fanny spends most of her time indoors, looking after his mother, and buys her a horse so she may go riding. Tom returns from Antigua without Sir Thomas; he explains that business is not going well, and he will be abroad much longer than expected. When Maria becomes engaged to the very rich, but stupid, Mr Rushworth, Sir Thomas sends his consent from Antigua.

Not long after Fanny turns 18, Dr Grant and Mrs Grant receive some visitors: Henry and Mary Crawford, Mrs Grant's siblings. Henry is not handsome, but he is the heir to a large estate, and his quick conversation and expert flirting soon attract both Julia and Maria. Mary is dainty, beautiful and talented. She is very charming and takes an immediate fancy to Tom, who will inherit Mansfield Park. Henry, on the other hand, spurns marriage – but Mrs Grant hopes that he will shortly change his mind and propose to Julia. Henry himself prefers Maria, despite – or rather, because of – her engagement to Mr Rushworth. The Bertrams and Crawfords quickly become close friends, though Henry and Mary find Fanny somewhat mysterious; they assume she is simply not 'out' in society yet, during a conversation in which it becomes apparent that none of the Bertrams has considered Fanny's being 'out' or not.

Tom soon leaves Mansfield again, this time to visit his wayward friends. Mary is disappointed, expecting Edmund – as the younger brother – to offer her no attraction. However, as they become better acquainted, they grow fond of each other.

When Mary tells Edmund of the difficulty she has encountered getting her harp delivered to the Grants' house (it is nearly harvest time, and she does not understand the social faux pas she has committed by expecting farmers to lend her a cart), Edmund notices her impropriety but finds himself falling in love with her. He discusses her with Fanny the next day; although he is pleased to find Fanny has also noticed Mary's flaws, he remains besotted with her.

Fanny herself is troubled by the blossoming friendship between Edmund and Mary. She has been in love with Edmund for years and is threatened by Mary's beauty and alarmed at her loose speech. Edmund offers Mary the use of the horse which he bought for Fanny; soon she is riding it every day, leaving Fanny trapped with Lady Bertram and Mrs Norris. Eventually, Edmund discovers that Fanny has become ill after spending a day running errands in the hot sun for her aunts. He is angry with himself for neglecting Fanny through his attentions to Mary, and is determined to make things up to her. His opportunity comes when the party arranges a trip to Sotherton, the estate of Mr Rushworth.

Because there is not enough room for everyone in the carriages, Mrs Norris insists that Fanny stay at Mansfield to look after Lady Bertram. Edmund challenges her, claiming that he will stay at home so that Fanny can go. Eventually, Mrs Grant offers to stay with Lady Bertram, and Edmund and Fanny are both permitted to join the outing.

The journey is fraught with tension. Julia and Maria, despite the latter's engagement, are fighting for Henry's affection, and when he picks Julia to sit beside him as he drives the carriage, Maria is angry. She comforts herself by bragging about Sotherton, which will be her home once she is married. Fanny has rarely left Mansfield since joining the household and is delighted merely by looking out of the carriage window. When the party arrives, they are given a tour of the estate by Mr Rushworth's mother. Fanny is surprised to discover that the chapel is a small and plain room. She voices her surprise to Edmund, sparking a debate between Edmund and Mary Crawford about the priesthood. Mary, unaware that Edmund intends to become a clergyman, is disparaging of the profession and claims that "in those days [when the chapel was first built], I fancy parsons were very inferior even to what they are now" (p. 82). She is embarrassed when Julia later remarks that it is a shame Edmund has not yet taken orders, otherwise he could marry Maria and Mr Rushworth that moment.

The group goes for a walk around the grounds: Maria, Henry and Mr Rushworth form one party, while Fanny, Edmund and Mary form a second. Julia is left with Mrs Norris and Mrs Rushworth. Fanny is largely left out of Edmund and Mary's conversation and when she grows tired, she is left by herself as the pair explores further. She is soon joined by Maria, Henry and Mr Rushworth. They try to go through a gate to reach the rest of the park, but the gate is locked. Mr Rushworth is persuaded to rush back to the house and fetch the key. While he is gone, Maria and Henry pass through the railings and go off alone, despite Fanny's warnings. Julia arrives, furious to discover her sister is alone with Henry. She follows them. Finally, Mr Rushworth returns. He is upset that the rest of the party has gone off without him and quizzes Fanny about Henry, clearly suspicious of his behaviour.

Shortly after the trip to Sotherton, the Bertrams receive a letter from Sir Thomas, informing them that he will return home in November. Maria, keenly aware that her father's return will prompt her marriage to Rushworth, hopes he will be delayed. Mary is also dreading Sir Thomas's reappearance, as it means Edmund will take his priestly orders. She teases him at a party one evening, describing Dr Grant – who is also a clergyman – as "an indolent selfish Bon vivant, who must have his palate consulted in every thing" (p. 104). Fanny is appalled at Mary's ingratitude towards Dr Grant.

LOVERS' VOWS

Tom soon returns to Mansfield again. Mary finds him repellent and the contrast between the Bertram brothers cements her preference for Edmund. Tom brings a friend with him, Mr Yates, who proves himself to be selfish and improper; he talks of a play in which he had been acting before coming to Mansfield, regretting the fact that the performance had never taken place – the host's grandmother had died before rehearsals ended. Tom is excited by the story and suggests they put on a play at Mansfield Park. Edmund and Fanny are strongly opposed, believing the theatricals will open up the family to gossip and scorn. Heedless to their concerns, Tom begins to construct a theatre in Sir Thomas's private rooms.

The group eventually chooses to perform *Lovers' Vows*, a play written by Elizabeth Inchbald in 1798. (It proved popular but was controversial thanks to its themes of illegitimacy and seduction). Julia is furious when Henry picks Maria to act the part of Agatha, his love interest. She correctly sees this as confirmation that he prefers her sister and refuses to have anything more to do with the play. There are eventually just two parts left to cast: Anhalt, a clergyman who marries Mary's character, Amelia, and a small female role. Tom asks Fanny to take this part; when she refuses, Mrs Norris attacks her, claiming "I shall think her a very obstinate, ungrateful girl [...] – very ungrateful indeed, considering who and what she is" (p. 137).

Upset, Fanny seeks refuge in the old nursery. Edmund arrives to ask for her advice. Despite his earlier protestations, he has decided to accept the role of Anhalt after all – for if he does not, Tom will recruit an outsider to play the part. Fanny is appalled and believes Mary has led Edmund astray. Meanwhile, as rehearsals get underway, it becomes apparent to everyone that Henry and Maria are attracted to each other. Fanny is pained watching Edmund and Mary together. Finally, the night of the dress rehearsal arrives – but proceedings are soon brought to a halt when Sir Thomas arrives home unexpectedly. As Edmund and Fanny anticipated, he is disapproving of the amateur theatricals and hastens Yates's departure. Fanny is surprised by the warmth with which her uncle greets her. Mrs Norris is displeased and attempts to get his good opinion for herself, telling Sir Thomas that she has looked after the family in his absence and secured Maria's engagement. Sir Thomas merely rebukes her for allowing the play to take place.

ONE WEDDING AND A PROPOSAL

Soon, Henry leaves for Bath, much to Maria's disappointment; she expected him to declare his love for her before departing. Her father has become concerned by her engagement to

Rushworth, who is obviously an idiot and not particularly well-liked by Maria. He offers to break off the engagement on his daughter's behalf – but Maria, embittered by Henry's neglect and eager to spite him, tells Sir Thomas that she does want to marry Rushworth. The wedding takes place quickly, and the couple, accompanied by Julia, leaves for Brighton.

With Maria and Julia gone, Fanny and Mary Crawford become closer. Fanny is invited to dine at the Grants' house with Edmund, and although Mrs Norris is appalled, Sir Thomas encourages Fanny to accept the invitation. He even insists that she travel by carriage – shocking both Fanny and Mrs Norris. When Edmund and Fanny arrive at the Grants', they are surprised to find that Henry has returned from Bath. They following day, Henry announces to Mary that he intends to make Fanny fall in love with him. Soon, however, Fanny's brother William – on leave from the Navy – comes to stay at Mansfield. Henry is touched by Fanny's devotion to her brother and decides that he is actually in love with her himself. He begins to woo her, much to Fanny's discomfort.

Sir Thomas announces his intention to throw a ball for Fanny and William. Edmund is also making plans: he will soon be ordained and has decided to propose to Mary. William gives Fanny an amber cross pendant to wear at the ball, but she has no chain to put it on. Mary offers to lend her one and once Fanny has accepted, Mary reveals the chain was a gift from Henry. Fanny tries to give it back, uneasy with Henry's recent attentions. When she arrives home, she finds Edmund in her room. He has brought her a gift: another chain that he has got for her cross. Later, he calls upon Mary at the parsonage to ask her to dance at the ball – but Mary insults him, claiming it will be the last time she dances with him, for she could never dance with a clergyman.

Dressing for the ball, Fanny is delighted to discover that the chain from Edmund fits the cross far better than the chain from Mary. Lady Bertram sends her own maid to help Fanny get ready. Although she is much too late, Fanny feels the kindness of the gesture. The ball itself is a great success. It is the first ball to be held at Mansfield, despite Maria and Julia's efforts to organise one, and Fanny feels part of the family at last.

The next day, William leaves Mansfield with Henry, who is taking him to meet his uncle who is an Admiral. Edmund also departs to take orders. With Julia still with Maria, Fanny becomes a favourite with Sir Thomas and Lady Bertram. Meanwhile, Mary is agonising over her treatment of Edmund. She regrets her disparagement of the clergy and, during a downpour of rain, visits Fanny in desperation to find out where Edmund is. She learns that Edmund is staying with a friend who has two eligible sisters. Fanny sees that Mary is distressed and trusts her feelings for Edmund are genuine.

That night, Henry returns to the parsonage and tells Mary that he is going to ask Fanny to marry him. Mary believes the marriage will help her chances with Edmund, while Henry is pleased that it will anger Maria and Julia. The next morning, he visits Fanny at Mansfield. He tells her that his uncle, the Admiral, has made William a lieutenant. Fanny is overwhelmed by the news and thanks Henry for introducing William. Henry seizes his chance and proposes marriage. He hands Fanny a letter from Mary, congratulating her on the engagement. Fanny is horrified and rejects Henry's offer. She is further aghast when Henry repeats the offer to Sir Thomas, who supports the match and is displeased that Fanny has refused it.

Having been ordained, Edmund returns to Mansfield. He is disappointed that Mary is still at the parsonage; he had hoped she would have left before he got back. Upon learning of Henry's proposal to Fanny, Edmund gently rebukes her for refusing him. Sir Thomas asks him to persuade Fanny to accept Henry – but Fanny does not change her mind and the Crawfords soon leave the parsonage. On leave from the Navy again, William returns to Mansfield. Sir Thomas presses Fanny to accompany her brother to Portsmouth when he goes to visit their parents; he feels that a reminder of her family's status will induce her to accept Henry's proposal. Fanny, who has not seen her parents since she left Portsmouth as a child, is happy to leave Mansfield – especially as Edmund has told her he plans to propose to Mary.

In Portsmouth, Fanny is dismayed by her family. Her father is coarse and rude, while her mother is too busy to spend time with her. She longs for Mansfield and, above all, Edmund. Only her 14-year-old sister Susan provides any respite. One day, to Fanny's surprise, Henry arrives in Portsmouth. He is introduced to the family as William's benefactor, having introduced him to the Admiral. He is invited to have dinner with the Prices that evening and Fanny is relieved when he does not accept – she is incredibly embarrassed by her vulgar and chaotic family. Fanny decides to educate Susan and worries about what will become of her after she returns to Mansfield.

RESOLUTION

Fanny receives a letter from Edmund, who has been in London with his sisters and Mary. He writes that he has returned home, disappointed to discover that Mary's friends in London are clearly bad influences. He is too in love with her to consider marrying anyone else and regrets that Fanny's marriage to Henry – which he views as inevitable – will make his relationship with Mary more difficult. He also states that, although everyone misses her, Sir Thomas will not be able to send for Fanny until after Easter. She soon receives another letter, this time from Lady

Bertram, who informs her that Tom is seriously ill. Excessive drink has left him near death, and he is currently being nursed at Mansfield.

When a third letter arrives, it is from Mary. Fanny is appalled by Mary's claim that Tom's death would benefit her, since Edmund would then inherit the estate. She is surprised to receive yet more correspondence from her which warns her not to believe any rumours she hears concerning Henry and Maria. Later that day, Fanny is sitting with her father who – as always – is reading the newspaper. It mentions a scandal in the Rushworth household: "Mrs R" has eloped with "Mr C."

Fanny soon hears from Edmund, who is on his way to Portsmouth to bring Fanny – and Susan, if she wishes – back to Mansfield. He brings yet more bad news: Julia has also eloped, with Mr Yates. Edmund arrives the next day, clearly in turmoil. When they arrive home, Lady Bertram is delighted to have Fanny back and tells her that Sir Thomas has learnt of Maria and Henry's flirtations. To his dismay, the scandal has made a marriage between Edmund and Mary impossible. Edmund reveals that he went to see Mary as soon as he learnt of his sister's disappearance and was distraught by her attempts to justify their elopement. Fanny tells Edmund that Mary had hoped Tom would die and leave him the heir. Edmund says that he will never love another woman and that Fanny's friendship is all he needs now.

With Tom's recovery, life at Mansfield becomes more stable. Julia and Mr Yates have married and are welcomed back into the family. Fanny's companionship cheers Edmund, who quickly realises he is in love with her. Mary goes to live with the Grants, who move to Westminster, while Mrs Norris and Maria – who has been divorced by Mr Rushworth and abandoned by Henry – set up home together. Susan is delighted to be adopted by Lady Bertram. Fanny and Edmund are married and move into the parsonage at Mansfield Park, where they live very happily.

CHARACTER STUDY

FANNY PRICE

Fanny Price bears almost no resemblance to Austen's earlier heroine, the spirited Elizabeth Bennet. Reserved and unprepossessing, she is introduced to us through the appraisal of her wealthy relatives:

> "Fanny Price was at this time just ten years old, and though there might not be much in her first appearance to captivate, there was, at least, nothing to disgust her relations. She was small of her age, with no glow of complexion, nor any other striking beauty; exceedingly timid and shy, and shrinking from notice; but her air, though awkward, was not vulgar, her voice was sweet, and when she spoke, her countenance was pretty" (p. 13).

Just as this description shifts from dismissive to complimentary, so too does Fanny's appearance blossom over the course of the novel. Upon returning from Antigua, Sir Thomas is surprised to find her more beautiful than she was when he left, and Edmund embarrasses Fanny greatly by complimenting her figure. Fanny herself is far slower to recognise her beauty: when getting dressed for a ball, she merely "[does] not dislike her own looks" (p. 250).

Her character has proved far more controversial than her appearance. Various literary critics – and even Austen's own mother – have announced that they do not care for Fanny, describing her as "priggish" (Calvo, 2005) and even "a heroine who was not made to be loved" (Auerbach, 1980). However, there is an irony to Auerbach's claim. We learn from Austen's narrator that Edmund has both "formed [Fanny's] mind and gained her affections", meaning "he had a good chance of her thinking like him" (p. 61). The idea that Fanny and Edmund's compatibility stems from his formation of her mind suggests she has indeed been 'made' to be loved, for Edmund has sculpted her into his ideal woman.

EDMUND BERTRAM

Edmund Bertram – handsome, religious and dutiful – appears to be the picture of morality. Unswervingly concerned with doing the right thing, his kind nature is nevertheless tinged by a stubbornness which ultimately loses him Mary Crawford, the woman he thinks he loves:

> "The issue of all depended on one question. Did she love him well enough to forego what had used to be essential points – did she love him well enough to make them no longer essential?" (p. 236).

Edmund's refusal to marry Mary unless she changes her character is a particularly uncharitable gesture from someone who prides himself on fairness. While he is initially keen to excuse Mary's imperfections, his sudden decision to marry Fanny – a woman whose opinions never depart from his own – reveals his overwhelming intolerance.

MARY CRAWFORD

Mary Crawford is perhaps the typical Austen heroine – in everything besides the fact that, in *Mansfield Park,* she is the *anti*-heroine. Beautiful, dark-haired and dainty, it is Mary who makes what is perhaps the most explicit innuendo in any of Austen's novels, a reference to sodomy in the Royal Navy: "Certainly, my home at my uncle's brought me acquaintance with a circle of admirals. Of *Rears* and *Vices*, I saw enough. Now do not be suspecting me of a pun, I entreat" (p. 57).

Mary's coarse sense of humour is likely a result of her upbringing: like Fanny, she was brought up by relatives and bears the emotional scars of her childhood. However, unlike Fanny – whose claim that she "cannot act" (p. 135) seems to apply to her life as much as to *Lovers' Vows* – Mary is "not born to sit still and do nothing. If I lose the game it shall not be from not striving for it" (p. 224). The 'game', in *Mansfield Park*, has Edmund Bertram as the prize. Both women are in love with him, but Mary's cosmopolitan morals are ultimately irreconcilable with Edmund's Christian principles.

ANALYSIS

PLAYACTING

Mansfield Park questions the extent to which people play the social roles assigned to them. The amateur theatricals suggested by Mr Yates are more than an indiscretion; they are a literalisation of one of the key themes of the novel. When Fanny shrinks from the idea of taking part in the play, claiming that she cannot act, her statement is full of dramatic irony: after all, the play allows the characters to express themselves more openly than they are able to in everyday life, with the lines between art and reality becoming distinctly blurred. Julia learns the truth about Henry's intentions, for example, when he chooses Maria over Julia for the part of Agatha; in this case, the onstage romance reveals affections held offstage. Who, then, is acting more – the lovers who use theatre to indulge in real feelings? Or Fanny, whose inhibitions rise from the subordinate position she has been forced to fill since arriving at Mansfield Park?

Henry Crawford finds the distinction between acting and honesty even harder to find. The fact he is described as a good actor has an obvious double meaning: the romantic role he plays onstage is one he also plays in everyday life, through his relentless attempts to make women fall in love with him. When he reads to Lady Bertram from a volume of Shakespeare, this skill is again made obvious:

> "[Fanny] could not abstract her mind five minutes; she was forced to listen; his reading was capital, and her pleasure in good reading extreme. To good reading, however, she had long been used; [...] but in Mr Crawford's reading, there was a variety of excellence beyond what she had ever met with. The King, the Queen, Buckingham, Wolsey, Cromwell, all were given in turn; for with the happiest knack, the happiest power of jumping and guessing, he could always light, at will, on the best scene, or the best speeches of each; and whether it were dignity or pride, or tenderness or remorse, or whatever were to be expressed, he could do it with equal beauty. – It was truly dramatic" (p. 312).

Lady Bertram announces that hearing Henry read is "really like being at a play" (p. 313) – and indeed, she has just witnessed a piece of theatre, for Henry's reading is not mere entertainment, but an effort to impress Fanny and ultimately win her affections.

SLAVERY

The nature of Sir Thomas's business in Antigua is never explicitly divulged – but there is much to be inferred from the fact that Fanny's question about the slave trade (which was partially abolished in 1807) is followed by "a dead silence" (p. 184). While the 1999 film adaptation of *Mansfield Park* starring Frances O'Connor brings the theme of slavery right to the surface (Fanny hears the singing of slaves on a ship moored in Portsmouth harbour, and learns that Tom left Antigua because he could not bear his father's abuse of the slaves on his plantation), slavery in the novel is more subtly alluded to. The name 'Mansfield', for example, could be a reference to John Mansfield, the contemporary Lord Chief Justice in England who played an active role in the abolition of the slave trade. This would certainly be ironic if Sir Thomas is involved in the slave trade, as Mansfield Park – a modern estate – would have been built on proceeds from enslavement. Similarly, the name of Mrs Norris – a tyrannical bully – could have been inspired by Robert Norris, a prominent slave-trader who died in 1791.

The undertones of slavery provide a sinister flip-side to the lives of those at Mansfield Park. When Fanny receives chains from Henry and Edmund, we are reminded that a symbol of restraint can also be a symbol of love and bonding:

> "She had, to oblige Edmund, resolved to wear [Henry's chain] – but it was too large for the purpose. His therefore must be worn; and having with delightful feelings joined the chain and the cross, those memorials of the two most beloved of her heart, those dearest tokens so formed for each other by every thing real and imaginary – and put them round her neck, and seen and felt how full of William and Edmund they were, she was able without an effort to resolve on wearing Miss Crawford's necklace too" (p. 250).

Fanny's fastening of the chain around her neck recalls, perhaps, the grotesque practice of shackling slaves. Had she been forced to wear the Crawfords' chain only, it would have reinforced an old comparison between loveless marriage and slavery – something which women in Austen's era were often fully aware of.

BUILDINGS

Nobody is more aware than Maria that marriage can be a form of entrapment. The prospect of marrying Mr Rushworth is repellent, something symbolised by Austen's descriptions of Sotherton house – ironically, the one factor that endears the match to Maria. The design of the estate, which Rushworth is keen to improve, is apparently as daft as its owner:

> "The situation of the house excluded the possibility of much prospect from any of the rooms, and while Fanny and some of the others were attending Mrs Rushworth, Henry Crawford was looking grave and shaking his head at the windows. Every room on the West front looked across a lawn to the beginning of the avenue immediately beyond tall iron palisades and gates" (p. 80).

The poor view from the rooms of Sotherton, the couple's soon-to-be marital home, reflects the dead-end nature of Maria's marriage to Rushworth. Prison-like, the grounds are surrounded by "tall iron palisades and gates" which – finding them locked – Maria and Henry eventually climb over to escape into the avenue while waiting for Rushworth to provide the key. The house, with all its grandeur and social status, reflects the institution of marriage and the lack "of much prospect" which such a marriage as Rushworth's and Maria's must bring.

FURTHER REFLECTION

SOME QUESTIONS TO THINK ABOUT...

- Do you believe that Edmund is genuinely in love with Fanny by the end of the novel? Why, or why not?
- Maria's fate is an unhappy one. Does she deserve this? Why, or why not?
- What comment do you think Jane Austen is making about social class? Explain your answer.
- Do you think that Henry Crawford is evil, just bored, or both? Explain your answer.
- Sir Thomas is not particularly liked by his daughters and is disappointed by their behaviour. Do you think he is a good father? Why, or why not?
- What is the significance of the railings Maria and Henry climb over at Sotherton? What could they symbolise?
- How does the presentation of Fanny in film adaptations compare with her character in the

novel? Why do you think the directors have made these changes?

- Fanny is appalled by Mary's ingratitude towards Dr and Mrs Grant. What role does 'gratitude' play in the novel?

We want to hear from you!
Leave a comment on your online library
and share your favourite books on social media!

FURTHER READING

REFERENCE EDITION

- Austen, J. (2011) *Mansfield Park*. London: Penguin.

REFERENCE STUDIES

- Auerbach, N. (1980) Jane Austen's Dangerous Charm: Feeling as One Ought about Fanny Price. In: J. Todd ed., *Jane Austen: New Perspectives*. London. Holmes & Meier.

- Calvo, C. (2005) Rewriting Lear's Untender Daughter: Fanny Price as Regency Cordelia in Jane Austen's *Mansfield Park*. *Shakespeare Survey*. Vol. 58. Cambridge: Cambridge University Press.

- Milligan, I. (1988) *Studying Jane Austen*. London: Longman.

- Tandon, B. (2003) *Jane Austen and the Morality of Conversation*. London: Anthem Press.

ADAPTATIONS

- *Mansfield Park*. (1999) [Film]. Patricia Rozema. Dir. US: Miramax Films.

- *Mansfield Park*. (2007) [TV film]. Iain B. MacDonald. Dir. UK: ITV.

MORE FROM BRIGHTSUMMARIES.COM

- Reading guide – *Emma* by Jane Austen.
- Reading guide – *Northanger Abbey* by Jane Austen.
- Reading guide – *Persuasion* by Jane Austen.
- Reading guide – *Pride and Prejudice* by Jane Austen.
- Reading guide – *Sense and Sensibility* by Jane Austen.

www.brightsummaries.com

Ebook EAN: 9782808016353

Paperback EAN: 9782808016360

Legal Deposit: D/2018/12603/578

Cover: © Primento

Digital conception by Primento, the digital partner of
publishers.